QUICK FIX FOR ENHANCED LIFE JOURNEY

A BOOK WHICH CONTAINS 21 SECRET SAUCES TO LIVE A BETTER AND HAPPY LIFE.

MUSKAN RAJKOTIA

"I dedicate this book to all those who want to live a happy, finer and healthy life, but because of some things they are not able to always live happily."

Contents

Preface

"Hello Dear Readers,

How I got an idea to write this Book and what led me to write this book? So, I always wanted to make some positive change in others lives and also wanted to add some values in their lives. I wanted to be reason of someone's joy.

We all want to live a Good Life but are not able to due to some factors.

This book is a small step of mine for making people's lives more cheerful. This book contains some ways by which you can have a better and healthy living.

"

ACKNOWLEDGEMENTS

"Gratitude goes to my family who helped me to complete my Book and who are source of inspiration for me.

I am also Thankful to God for giving me strength to sucessfully write my first book.

Thanking You,

Muskan Rajkotia"

I

Why To Say- 'I Owe You One' ?

"We often complain for not having things that others do have. But, we should understand that our life may be a ***DREAM LIFE*** *for some other person livimg out there. You should know that, YOU ARE BLESSED for everything we got.*

We sometimes fail to say Thankyou and take things for Granted. If you want to be HAPPIER and SATISFIED in your Life, BE GRATEFUL. You must ***'Practice 'GRATITUDE daily.*** *People who APPRECIATE Little Things, are much more happier than others who don't practice gratitude.*

I OWE YOU ONE, is said to ***Thank SOMEONE you Helped You.*** *You should be GRATEFUL and THANKFUL, for every little things that we have got in our life. Learn to say THANKYOU.*

We usually go to restaurants or hotel and order food. But do you remember that how many times you had said Thankyou to the waiters or attendants who serves you the food? Thankyou is a small word, however it creates an impact. Do say Thankyou to them, it makes them feels good.

Another daily life example is our MOTHER. She cook food for us, BE GRATEFUL to them. When our mom cook tasty food, we generally say Tasty Food or Delicious Food. But very few are there who say, 'Thankyou Mom'. If till now you had not said Thankyou Mom to your mother, start saying this from today. It makes her feel special.

Now, you might be thinking that how we can appreciate things? So, lets see this below. ***1)****Go out for youself one day and pamper youself.* ***2)*** *Be Grateful in negative phase of your life also.* ***3)****Spend some timen with your friends and family.* ***4)****Greet everyday in your life with a smile and positivity.* ***5)*** *Celebrate mini wins in your life.*

Hence, ***focus on what you have and if you will appreciate things*** *that you have and are thankful for it, then you will surely get more.*

"

II

Come Out Social

"In this world, there are people who live a lavish life. While on the other hand, there are people who cannot fulfill even their basic needs. Poor people do not have enough food to eat, they cannot afford to have good and fancy food items, can't afford good clothes to wear, cannot afford to get admitted to rich and good schools, some are also forced to work at the age in which they should study to make a bright future.

As citizens, it's our liability to succour people of the society. If not always, atleast once or twice a week we shouls AID THE NEEDY.

There are many ways to assist the needy. Some are - ***1)*** *Providing them some of our old clothes ,* ***2)****Offering them home made lunch ,* ***3)*** *Many of us have domestic workers for our household works. We can pay their child's school, tuition or college fees.* ***4)****Celebrate your domestic workers special days like Birthday's, Anniversary etc. in a good manner,* *which becomes memorable for them.*

We must be **GIVERS.** *And should be* **PLEASED** *that we are that much capable that we can help out others.We all must inculcate the* PRACTICE OF SHARING. *Like, we can share our lunch box with our friends or colleagues. Sharing our pen with our friends, if they haven't bought etc.*

Sometimes buying Diya's during Diwali from small vendors and not from sizeable shops is also another way to be social. As, we should know that they are selling these to feed their family and are not in any competition of becoming the richest persons.

Those who are good persons and have good heart they know to help others and they in true sense help others.

So, Be Good and Be Social.
”

III

Are You Caught In The Cage Of Overthinking ?

"Do you think too much about any particular thing, my dear friend then you are thinking too much, which means you are overthinking. Overthinking is Injurious to Health. Overthinking is harmful for health and causes more stress. Overthinking is the cause of unhappiness.

What's the point to take so much of load and stress and to think too much?

For example, as a student we may be worry about getting good marks in exams, getting admission in top colleges, getting a good job etc.

We should not take stress and should live our lives happily. We have got just one life, so live it to the fullest. Thinking of having a good future is ok but remember do take too much of stress or don't overthink unnecesarily. Don't take tension for the things which does not even exists, because by taking tension nothing will become right.

Remember that, if it is in your destiny then surely you will get that no matter what, and if it is not in your destiny then whatever you do you will not get that. You will get things at the right time...not before the time and not after. Believe in God, that he has planned something big and great for you.

Now let's see some ways by which we can ***RELIEVE from Overthinking*** *1) Give up what makes your mind heavy* ***2)*** *Include Medidatation in your daily routine.* ***3)****Never Comapre youself with other's.* ***4)****When in Stress, Close your eyes...and take a deep breath.* ***5)*** *Take Rest for some time.*

So, for a happy life... just <u>*Go With The Flow.*</u> *And leave the things which you cannot control upon God. And just* <u>*Have Believe in the Process*</u> *. Hvae Faith that what is happening and what will happen in future will be Good and for your betterment and happiness.*

So, just promise to youself that from now onwards you will not take any kind of tension and will go with the flow."

IV

Relinquish the destroyer - EGO

"There are several factors that works like an obstacle in our success, and one of them is EGO. We should remember that there is difference between Self-Esteem and Self-Respect. In any kind of relationship, there should be SELF RESPECT and not EGO.

No relationship can last long if there is Ego. It's better to say Sorry and to lose your Ego to your loved ones, Then to lose your loved one. There's a difference between having Attitude and being an Egoistic Person. Higher the Ego, Lower the acceptance level.

Attitude is nature of a person that how he tackles any situation. Most of the times, situation is same but how we tackle it makes a difference. On the other hand, Ego is to take pride of your importance and how we see ourselves. While, Attitude is how we see other's and the situation. People always likes a person who has good attitude. However, people dislikes the one who is an Egoistic person.

An egoistic person always treats himselg superior then others. According to him, he is always on top no matter what. He don't understand others view point. He don't let other's to talk in any conversation. This creates a negative image of him in front of other's.

Now let's have a look that how we can give up Ego - **1)** *Accept yourself that who you are, and to find your true abilities .* **2)***Do something for the betterment of the society.* **3)***Meditate daily.* **4)***Be Grateful for what you have.* **5)***Do Forgive people.*

To live a respectful and cheerful life, having good and positive attitude is important and not to be an egoistic perosn. Just release your Ego and see how people gets attracted towards you and give you importance, respect and value.

"

V

Live In The Present

*"For a **Jovial and Cherry life**, one thing which is important is to - **LIVE IN THE PRESENTMOMENT.** Living in the Present can be described as - Not to Regret about the past and not to take Brood about the future. When we live in the present moment then our mind remains healthy.*

Everyone of us wants to live in the present, but are not able to because we worry about the future or have regret about the past. It's important to understand that Past is what is gone and cannot be changed whereas, future is not in our control and is the phase of our life which we have not seen yet. So, all we havc got is Present.

*Just **live in the present moment and see how ur life becomes smooth.** Life is there only at this moment ie., to say at the Present moment.*

*If you really want to live at the present moment, below are some tips for the same **1) Don't think much about your past as it's gone.** Past was the time in* *your life which is gone whereas the future is not-known to us. So, it's better to focus only on the present moment and to live it happily.*

2)Do not hold Grudges. *Life is there to live happily and not to hold any kind of grudges. So, spread love and spread smile.*

3)Be Greatful. *We should be grateful for what all we have in our lives. As well as we should appreciate things in our lives.*

4) Meditade daily *To keep our mind calm and to remain healthy from mind body and spirit, it is important to Medidate daily.*

So dear readers, from now onwards lets just go with the flow without regreting about past and without worrying about the future. Let focus on making our present the best and happiest day of our lives. And don't let the dejection and regret of your past to destroy your present moment."

VI

This Precious Time Will Not Come Back

"Time is the most valauble asset of our life. Once gone will not come back no matter how strongly you want the passed time to come back. People even after knowing that once the time is gone will not come again still waste their precious time.

Remember, if now you will waste your time, the only thing which will be left with you is Regret. It's better to work hard now, then to cry for the same thing later.

*Some ways that you can productively use your valuable time are given below - **1)Create a TO DO LIST** Before sleeping, just plan your next day well in advance so that their is no wastage of time for preparing the tasks that you have to do throughout* *your day.*

2) Eat healthy and stay Fit *Do eat healthy food and do exercise so that your energy level to do your work remains high and your mind remains healthy and sharp.*

3)Don't say Yes Always *Above all, just remember that your time is precious. Before completing your To Do tasks which you have planned for the day, donot hangout out or enjoy with your friends. If your friends say you to join them in any celebration or enjoyment and your work is pending, Learn to say NO to them.*

4)Prioritize your tasks *From all the works that to perform in your day, prioritize all your works."*

VII

Be a Reason Of Someone's Joy

"We should be the reason of someone's joy and smile. If you want to live a happy life,then make someone's life Good and cheerful. We should be grateful that we are that fortunate to make someone life better.

If someone is sad and you make him/her happy, then you have done the great thing. Making happy to someone is a work which everyone cannot do. If you are happy then you can keep other's also happy.

We should be such a kind hearted person that after seeing you or after talking with you brings smile on their face and with whom everyone likes to talk.

I just like to share with you all one small and recent incident of mine. During the days of Diwali 2021, I thought to distribute some food items to the needy people. After distributing them, the smile that

I saw on their faces was unparallel. That smile and happiness on their face made me much happier.

We should always try to be a contributor of someone's happiness and joy."

VIII

Develop The Habit Of Reading

*"Reading is the best habit that one should inculcate in their daily routine. You must read **minimum 20-30 minutes daily**. Many people out there, have reading habits which is the Best habit to adopt.*

Reading aid you to succeed in life. There are soo many books which are available in the market, and each book have somthing to teach you. It also helps us to become a good human being.

Benefits of reading** - **1)**It improves your writing skills and vocabulary. **2)**When you are tired, books helps you to reduce stress and worries. **3)** It increases your communication skills as we come across various new words while reading. **4)** Reading makes us more knowledgable person. **5)**We become aware about what is happening in our surroundings. **6)**Reading makes us more creative person. **7)

Reading helps us to make our mind healthy. ***8)*** *Reading also keeps us motiovated and positive.*

So, ***Keep Reading Keep Learning New Things.***"

IX

Put An End To Excuses

“Excuses means, to give the grounds that you are ineffective and incapable to do that tasks or work. Excuse acts a hurdle in the path of your success. Everyone wants to be rich, want to be sucessfull in their lives, want high paying job, good lifestyle etc etc., but for all these comes the hardwork, action, ability to take risk and No Excuses.

If you are making excuses then you are allowing someone else to become more successful then you. Also you are allowing them to take the opportunity available, which you could have grabed if not made excuses.

Before accepting any task, some people usually say - < I don't have resources to execute it. < I'm ungifted to do this piece of work. <I'm a defeated person.

So, for a better living, remember that ***you alone are answerable for the happenings in your life.*** *Your future is in your hands, stop making excuses and msake better version of your life.*

Also, ***don't blame other's*** *instead learn take that responsibility or charge that it's only you that can make a finer version of your life.*

Remember, it's perpetually Now. ***To achieve your big dreams, Put an end to Excuses.*** ”

X

Don't Be Judgemental

"In today's world, people Judge others very easily. We should not form our own schhol of thought about someone without knowing them nicely. Also we should not form our opinion or belief for something only on the basis of how it looks to us.

Usually people love those who are rich or good looking. People love to judge others and even to those to who they don't know nicely. If we judge anyone then this shows that we don't respect that perosn. And we know that, if we want respect from others then first learn to give respect to others.

If we judge the person, can break our relations with them. Before making any opinion for someone just remember, that you are still unaware of his/her struggles or helplessness of them.

For example, if anyone has dark color then people judge them easily. If someone's height is small or is not physically or mentally fit people make fun of them.

But do remember its not always the appearence that is to be seen. Appearence and looks are secondary and what is more important is the way they respects you, how loyal he/she is for you and how he/she treats you.

Passing negative judgements for something or someone shows that we are not well mannered and what kind of values we have got."

XI

Why Resisting Change? Adopt It

"Want an easy going life?....then, don this. People who are successful, accept the change and goes according to time. Change, though the word is small...but it's importance in our lives is quite big.

The ones who resist change donot grow in their lives. All the excitment and adventure from their lives vanishes.

Change occures in every sphere of life. If we keep living all the days in the same manner as the previous ones, then our life will become monotonous. So, <u>to add some spark of adventure and excitment in our life, change is very important.</u>

You never know, when and how your habit of accepting and embracing the change can ***bring opportunities in your lives.***

Trying different things, sometimes lands you to ***find your passion.***

If you don't know how ***strong personality you are****, then do admit changes in your life.*

So, do take on and adopt the change, and explore new things and people."

XII

Comparision Isn't Always Fruitful

*"<u>One of the root cause of our saddness is</u> **<u>Comparision.</u>** Comparision from others...from the outside world. But just tell me, with how many people you can compare yourself. Why do we compare ourselves from others. We don't know how their life journey and how our life journey will be.*

For example, if you are earning annual package of Rs. 20Lakhs. You are jubilant. But when you come to know that your friend is earning an annual package of Rs. 25Lakhs, then instead of being happy for him you will be downhearted.

If we take comparision as a stimulatin, then it can be fruitful otherwise quit harmful for you.

<u>Comparing the 6th chapter of your life with someone's 60th chapter,</u> ***will always gives you disappoinments and will break your self***

confidence.

When we compare ourselves and our lives with others, we are disrespecting ourselves and our talents. Just don't see that he/she is good at those things also see at your talents and how capable you are to do the things.

<Focus on your abilities, talents and strenghts.

<Take comparision as a source of stimulation.

< Focus on Good things of your life.

For Growth and happiness in life, compare your today with your yesterday.”

XIII

Respect All & Love All

*"'Respect' - The thing which we all want to get but everyone don't get. Respect is very important in any relationship. Its the **essence** of any relationship. Acceptance towards any person for who they are. If you are kind to others then you respect them.*

*Respect is **highly important in any relationship**, as it **builds the trust** in that relationship. Trust is very important to run the relationship. But dear all, respect should not be only be One-Sided but **should be Mutual.***

*If we will give Respect to others then only we should expect other's also to respect us. It doesn't matter that the other person is younger or elder to you, **Learn to Give Respect To All.***

Why we should give Respect to others ? i)** To get respect from someone, learn to give respect. **ii)** It sense* *of goodness in other's mind.* ***iii) *Shows that you are a well mannered person.* ***iv)*** *Works as a fuel to run the vehicle name- Relationship.*

Learn to show Respect to other's. Now let's see ***how we can show Respect to others*** *with some ways-*

1) *Be a good listener.* ***2)*** *Be Polite with other's.* ***3)****Be happy on their wins.* ***4)****Be a helping hand for other's.* ***5)****Understand other person's thoughts.* ***6)****Work for betterment of society.* ***7)****Serve the poor and needy.* ***8)****Accept your mistakes and say Sorry when you're incorrect.*

Another important thing is to LOVE ALL. Don't be judgemental. Don't love anyone only on the basis of their appeareance and looks. Instead love all. We should understand that everyone is a different person, have some uniqueness and goodness.

When you love anyone without expecting anything in return or ***without any expectations*** *from them then you Love All.*

When you Love all, it ***gives peace of mind.*** *Although it is difficult to love them who had done something wrong with us, but we should love them also.*

Donot limit your love to just handful of people, instead ***have an open heart to love all.***

Atlast, ***It's just One Life that we have got so, Spread Love Spread Happiness and Give Respect !"***

XIV
Ban Complaining

"Want a peaceful mind and peaceful life....then stop the habit of complaining. Don't always see bad things in person instead see good things in him or her. If you stop complaining, then there will a constructive impact on your life. It will ***keep your mind cool and calm.***

Complaining is always a ***waste of your precious time.*** *People also don't like those who always tends to complain. Instead be thankful for what you have with you in your life.*

Once you ***turn the habit of Complaining to the habit of being Thankful****, then it will be very smooth for you to live your life happily and also you can use your time in more productive activities and work.*

So, for a happy living, let the habit of complaining come to an end."

XV

Stop Procrastination From Becoming Your Habit

"Occasionally, we all had procrastinated some things in our lives. Even today many of us continue doing the same.

We procrastinate things because,<it seems monotonous to us. <You sometimes lack the reason of doing things.<You may get distracted from your goals.

If you are able to head your time judiciously, then you can vacate procrastination. For, this you can ***Make To Do list*** *for the next day before sleeping at night. This will help you utilise your time in more productive work and not to simply waste it by* *thinking that what you will do in your entire day.*

*If in a true way you are **dedicated and passionate towards your work and are concerned for your future** and of getting your dream job, you can beat procrastination.*

If, you don't feel to do your work or lack motivation to do it, just Think that Why you had started that. Also, think about the things that you will get once you will achieve your targets and how happy your life will be.

So, my dear readers, don't think too much and just start without any dely."

XVI

Control Your Anger

*"**Anger - The Enemy** of your "**health and relations**".If you are angry, you are making a negative environment. Like, throwing of garbage pollutes the environment, likewise anger pollutes our health, relations and many things.*

People who have fear of anything, stress or any issues in their lives shows anger. People also don't like such perosn's who always stays in an angry mood and who don't have smile on their face.

***If you are Angry, try the below listed tips.** **1)** Walk out for sometime from that place. **2)**Donot react too quickly. As some people when are angry, they don't know what they are saying to the other person. It's better not to react at that very moment. **3)** Find out the reasons because of which you are/were angry. As, sometime what happens is when we are angry that time we think that this is the big issue. But after sometime when our mind cools down and become calm we feel like - Oh No how foolish I am.*

That was not that big issue. ***4)*** *Practice Meditation, as it will help you to remain cool and calm in such situations.* ***5)*** *Excercise daily.* ***6)****Be a solution oriented person. Always look into the best possible solutions so that the matter can be dissolved.*

Don't let you Anger destroy your health and relations.

It's better to let go your Anger for your health and loved ones."

XVII

Release Your Past

"Past, sometimes makes us happy sometimes not. Some people always live in the past knowing that it is not fruitful for them. Past is what is gone and will come back. You can only learn from the mistakes which you have done in the past, and try no to repeat the same again.

If you are living in the past, then when you will live in the present?

Sometimes because of people we remain stuck in our past and sometimes because of some memories, whether happy or sad. But do remember, that time will not get stuck at one place because you don't want to move forward in your life.

Being physically present in the present moment but mentally in your past will fetch you nothing.

So, now lets see that how we can come out from our past. ? ***1)*** *Keep yourself busy with some productive work.* ***2)*** *Practice Meditation* ***3)****Work upon your Self Growth.* ***4)*** *Focus on self-care.* ***5)****Focus* *only on Positive things and not on negative one's.*

Stop wasting your time thinking or regretting about the past, instead move on and focus on your present.

My dear friend, your beautiful future is waiting for you so, ***Do Move Forward in your life and make your happy future.***

"

XVIII

Learn New Things Each Day

"Want Growth in your life? If your answer is Yes, then you are reading the correct sauce for better living. In today's competitive world, if you want to be remarkable then my dear friend keep learning new things each day, keep working upon your skills, be empathetic and enhance your skills.

There are so many things so learn these days. And we know that what we learn never go waste, as it will be fruitful and will help you in your future.

Some people only focus on becoming a perfectionist and don't want to try in any other area of work. . Being a perfectionist is good, but restricting yourself to not to work in any other field of work is definetly not a good choice. It will hamper your extension, which is not good for you.

As, a car cannot run without wheels, so we also cannot grow without swotting new things. Learning helps you to ***become more knowledgeable person****. If you want to improve your life journey in a positive manner, then do keep learning new things.*

Now, lets dive into the benefits of learning new things - ***1)*** *It also helps you to succeed in your life.* ***2)*** *Aid you to upgrade your life journey.* ***3)*** *Makes us more cheerful in our life.* ***4)*** *It's also connected with growth ie., you can also get higher pay in your job or can even get better job role.*

No matter what your age is or how old are you, but you should never end the process of learning."

XIX

Want Growth In Life? Then Quit This Habit

"We all have habbits, some good whereas some habits are bad. Our bad habits becomes obstacles in the road of our success. It is also harmful for our health. Your good habits provides benefit to you but, bad habits act like the hurdles in your life.

For example, when someone is depressed, then they usually end up consuming alcohal or do smoking which is injurious to health. It's a bad habit which you should stop if you also do the same in this situation.

If you also want to quit your bad habits, one way is to ***quit your bad habits with your friend circle.*** *For example, if you have a bad habit of not exercising then, you can start exercising with your friends so* *that soon your bad habit turns up to the mark.*

Another way, is by ***giving reward to yourself****. For example, you decided to quit any of your bad habit*

Third way ***Have Patience*** *- Don't think that you can break your bad habits in just 1 or 2 days..NO. As we know that it takes 21 days to break any habit or to built any habit.*

The last one is to **Opt Meditation***- Practice meditation atleast for 30 minutes a day to stay mentally and emotionally fit. As, it can reprogram the course of action you react to any affairs and sitch.*

It's better to replace your bad habits into good habits for a finer life.

So, dear readers after reading this sauce for better living, do promise that today you will quit any of your bad habit and replace it with high minded one.

"

XX

Cut Down Yourself With Toxic People

"For a happy Life and Mind, Staying positive is Important. But we cannot remain positive if we are surrounded by negative people. Negative people brings negative vibes and negative energy which is not good for us.

Spend time with the ones who makes you feel comfortable and with whom who love to talk. In our lives, we have to deal with people who gives us stress and by talking with them our mind gets occupies with negative thoughts.

If you are ATTACH with people who brings Stress and negative vibes in your life, then do detach yourself from such people as they are not good for your health.

When we talk with someone, do listen them and show interest in them. ***There are people who only***

talk about their problems and worries. *They never have smile on their face. When we talk with them, they only share their issues which they are facing in their lives. They generally focus on themselves .* ***All such negative talks makes are mind exhausting.***

To feel good and happy, it is better to ***detach yourself from such people who always bring negativity*** *in your life and mind. You can also* ***jump on to another topic*** *or* ***simply ignore their words,*** *so that your mind don't feel heavy.*

If you really want to be happy then ***stay away from such people.*** *It's Better to* ***surrond yourself with positive people*** *and who brings happiness in you life no matter if they are only handful, then having more people in your life out of which majority are the ones who creates stress in your life.*

You need to try to be less attached to people or things which gives us pain and makes us feel uncomfortable. As, our mental peace and happiness is upto us only."

XXI

Be Happy In Success Of Others

"Jealousy is an 'EMOTION' which can be POSITIVE or NEGATIVE. If we take jealousy as a fuel which keeps us motivated to work hard and to achieve something big in our lives, then it is positive jealousy. On the other hand, when people start comparing ourselves with others it becomes negative jealousy. ***COMPARISION is the main reason of negative jealousy.***

Nowadays, people usually become jealous of others happiness and success. In today's world, people are so much active on various social media platforms like- Instagram, Facebook, Snapchat, Whatsapp etc., that they share every bit of their life. Reels are becoming much popular these days. But my dear friend, why we are resentful of other's lives. It"s not always true what is been shown on social media platforms. We are not aware of the true picture, that what is happening in their lives.

Jealousy leads to ***depression and frustration.*** *When good things happens in other's lives we tend to become jealous due to insufficiency.*

Stop getting JEALOUS from others ***good fortune, success and happiness.*** *We don't know that what is their lives journey, how the journey of their life going to be and what God has planned for them.*

"

Conclusion

"For a fruitful and Joyful living, 21 tips (some do and some dont's) are given in this book. These are some tips which if implemented my you in your life, can change your life in a positive way.

Love Yourself, Love Others and Spread Happiness.

Wishing you all a Happy and Healthy Life Journey ahead !"

Printed by Libri Plureos GmbH in Hamburg,
Germany